Data Quality for Decision Makers

Guilherme Morbey

Data Quality for Decision Makers

A dialog between a board member
and a DQ expert

Second Edition

Guilherme Morbey
Erkrath, Germany

ISBN 978-3-658-01822-1   ISBN 978-3-658-01823-8 (eBook)
DOI 10.1007/978-3-658-01823-8

The Deutsche Nationalbibliothek lists this publication in the Deutsche Nationalbibliografie; detailed bibliographic data are available in the Internet at http://dnb.d-nb.de.

Library of Congress Control Number: 2013935128

Springer Gabler
© Springer Fachmedien Wiesbaden 2011, 2013

Printed on acid-free paper

Springer Gabler is a brand of Springer DE.
Springer DE is part of Springer Science+Business Media.
www.springer-gabler.de

Many thanks for suggestions and contributions specially to Hubert Wolken (Head of the BI Center, insurance company), Dr. Stephan du Carrois (Chief IT Architect, insurance company), Andrew Tatam (IT Management Consultant), Dr. Marcus Gebauer (Head of Data Management, re-insurance company), Annalee Elman (Data Architect Consultant), Sahri Morbey and Brigitte Habermann-Morbey (both psychologists with an in-depth statistical background) as well as

to all those

who got to know me as a consultant and became friends.

Thank you!

Foreword

Let Guilherme Morbey take you on an interesting journey to Data Quality. In the course of a fictional conversation between a consultant and a board member you will learn about the essentials of Data Quality and Data Quality Management. The conversation might take place any time as described or in a very similar fashion. And who knows, maybe it has already occurred.

In an entertaining and meaningful way you will find out how Data Quality can be installed in a technically safe way to support company goals. In the course of this unfolding story will become obvious that Data Quality is an indispensable necessity. And this is not only so because regulatory requests regarding Data Quality appear increasingly on the agenda.

Guilherme Morbey outlines what Data Quality is, how and in which dimensions it is measured reasonably, and how Data Quality measurement can be integrated into existing control mechanisms and into the entire company context. Furthermore he emphasizes that Data Quality should not only be measured, but that Data Quality, including all pertaining processes, should also be properly managed within the organisational set up. It is quite obvious that in traditional companies with their long established lines of action this will bring about some internal frictions. A glance at the success factors tops off the conversation.

Dr. Marcus Gebauer
Deutsche Gesellschaft für Informations- und Datenqualität (DGIQ e.V.)
(German Association for Information- and Data Quality)

Table of Contents

Figures and Tables

Prologue

Just imagine: You are a decision maker and want to understand what Data Quality (DQ) or Data Quality Management (DQM) is. You would like to know whether it is worthwhile to support activities headed in this direction and which are the essential success factors for your company. After a fruitless attempt to grasp the topic with the help of some slides in a meeting, you hope – just as I do – that the information in this booklet will help you.

To spice up a dry topic and present it in a livelier way, essential information contents are presented as a fictional dialogue between a corporate decision maker and an external consultant. The dialog addresses questions, objections and concerns that DQ consultants actually have to deal with in their daily work.

The starting scenario: At a financial service provider firm, there has been an ongoing controversial discussion about the meaning and value of DQ. Topics like "who is responsible for DQ" and "whether, when and to which extent DQ has to be attended to" have been discussed, with no conclusions having been reached. The Data Warehouse (DWH) division and the Business Intelligence Division had previously repeatedly tried to promote a DQ-related project, but it always had to be put on hold due to more urgent and demanding projects. It seemed that nobody was willing to spend time, budget or energy on DQ issues, especially since it would not pave the way for more contracts nor contribute to a concrete reduction of costs.

Nowadays, however, national and European authorities intervene and announce that they will soon demand "DQ Statements". As you can imagine, reactions in the company are manifold: spreading panic, a wondrous multiplication of wise guys who already know everything about DQ, and the appearance of the nay-sayers, who state that DQ merely is a campaign of external consultants to fill new skins with old wine and that everything could be handled as before.

In this situation a member of the board of directors gets the vague feeling that previously involved departments might not have evaluated the topic of DQ to its full extend and cannot cope with it adequately due to their other important commitments. It is about time to have a detailed conversation with his old friend, an external consultant and a highly experienced project manager.

The consultant has been known to perform tasks objectively and fairly. Although he closely sticks to an exact and matter-of-fact approach, he is far from being a pedantic bookkeeper. Usually he engages people with his enthusiasm, wins them over to common objectives, and passionately defends concepts and projects.

The director or board member, introduced as a dialog partner, has, in the past, driven some successful IT projects, but is technically on the business track. From his colleagues he learns that specialists and managers have lately come to increasingly appreciate his friend's expertise regarding DQ. The director decides to contact him and hopes their conversation will not become bogged down in technical jargon.

His secretary arranges an open-end meeting for the late afternoon in a restaurant both frequently visited in the past.

1　Data Quality in General

At the appointed time they first meet at the manager's office. It is up to your imagination to picture the cultivated ambience and the old friends' convivial greeting ritual. Both quickly get down to business.

The consultant starts with an analogy.[1]

Before we face the topic of Data Quality (DQ), I would like to draw a comparison between data and water. In many cases it facilitated mine and my previous clients' understanding of important relationships.

1.1　Data is the water in the world of information

In the world of information data resembles the water, which we need in our everyday lives. In both worlds we talk about sources, supply chains, filters, processing plants, about owners and users. In water-works, for instance, we meet engineers who take care of the water transport, canals, pools, water pressure, water level and flow velocity. With regard to security, the engineers mainly control for unauthorized inflows and runoffs.

If one includes water quality inspectors, the picture gets even more complex. The water quality inspectors raise an alarm as soon as their measures at fixed places do not meet the agreed standards of water quality.

---

[1] Following up, the consultant's lines are indented. Contributions and questions from the manager are written in an italic font and aligned left.

1.2   Data Quality (Definition)

All right, that's an appealing analogy. Now let's become more concrete. What is Data Quality?

Data Quality refers to the degree of fulfilment of all those requirements defined for data, which is needed for a specific purpose.

This implies that comprehensible statements about the quality of the data can be made only after appropriate requirements for the data are formulated, and their compliance is systematically documented!

You will most certainly tell me in the course of our discussion how long it took you to find this handy and concise definition! Please write it down for me, so I can reconsider it once in a while. It might be true, but ...

1.3   We are already doing so much for Data Quality!

We have made high investments in standard applications, in the programming of millions of plausibly checks into each application, in process security, and in Data Transfer (ETL-programming[2]). Our organisational security follows international standards, we have organisation handbooks, and work groups for the standardisation of central data elements. We provide training and work instructions to our staff. Isn't that sufficient to provide DQ? Is there really anything else to do?

Everything you mention is doubtless an essential contribution to DQ. First and foremost these things guarantee the functioning of the whole system. If we stick to the analogy of the water supply, you have a well-functioning infrastructure with several water sources, splendidly

---

[2] ETL = Extract Transform and Load

constructed water runways and excellent filter equipment. But can you really operate it without using analytical chemists and water quality checks?

What about the external certified accountants, internal auditors and risk managers? We already involve so many people and conduct various crosschecks.

Indeed, these persons represent a highly educated specialist group, which knows much about data, especially about aggregated financial data. The data usually is interpreted and corrected in various regards (reconciliation/adjustment postings) until at a given call date it presents an acceptable and harmonic overall picture for a certain purpose. Thereby the exhausting data-related parts of the job are finished.

These procedures are repeated periodically; however, they might not have any effect on the condition of the DQ in the company! The "felt Data Quality" regularly is regarded as positive or as only marginally improvable. Apart from the "felt DQ" nothing more substantial can be presented. The reason for this is that there are neither any well-founded statements about DQ - based on predefined criteria - for periodical reports, nor any of the de facto necessary listings of deviations.

In our company we do not really understand what DQ is good for. If a significant data discrepancy is detected in a report or table, it is traced back. Either there was a miscalculation or initially false data was processed, or some other incident occurred. Afterwards the calculations are corrected, new data is uploaded or a recorded adjustment posting is carried out. We will continue to handle problems this way, won't we?

Yes, and it is good to have this option for exceptional cases. But here is what is going to happen in a correctly functioning DQ System: A

DQ deficiency will be detected not just accidentally, but automatically, as early as possible, and as close to the error source as possible, where it will be repaired within an acceptable time. With that approach, in the case of an error as few people as possible are involved. Defects are removed early and effectively, data consistency is ensured beyond departments, and the majority of the data reconciliations are dispensable. Wouldn't that be quite an advantage for a large company?

The currently implemented plausibility checks for entering data as well as the surveys in the transfer interfaces already assure consistent data, don't they?

Experiences gained from data analysis show that this is, diplomatically speaking, not always a safe assumption. Even without systematic analysis, there is much evidence emphasizing the problem. It comes from migration projects and interfaces to data warehouse systems as well as from the generation of controlling reports.

1.4   Benefits

What are the benefits of Data Quality Statements?

1. For the data entry responsible, DQ statements provide on the one hand a statistical value, which represents the quality level of the data and on the other hand detailed information about datasets conflicting with predefined requirements. The supervisor in charge may then correct these data quality deviations.

   After an initial data analysis the focus should in principle be upon the survey of data defects, which have not been detected by the previous plausibility checks of the application.

I have not yet found this functionality as a part of business software solutions.

2. Less DQ defects imply less internal friction for cooperation within a company. Good DQ positively affects all business processes and business fields. In any case, it contributes to a reliable basis for business decisions and causes much less work with data corrections at a later date.

3. With information about DQ, the different user circles such as management, internal data users, customers, investors, ranking agencies and regulators gain a good indicator if and to which extent their data-based statements may be trusted. Information about DQ is an invaluable signal of confidence for internal use and for the external image of a company.

Please allow me just one question: Assume you have the chance to choose between two comparable and well-established water suppliers. Both receive their water from an approximately 400 km distant source. It is assured that the water quality of both suppliers is good. One of them can provide evidence by chemical analyses and has a well-established system of quality controls along the water pipes. The other refers to his long tradition, the large number of customers, and the fact that nothing adverse has ever happened before. When the latter is asked about chemical analysis of the water quality, he replies that there have never been any complaints and that there has never been a need for such checks. Now, which supplier would you choose?

You are certainly not expecting an answer; it's just too obvious. Is there a way to quantify the benefit?

Yes, absolutely. Before the start of a project, however, it is exceedingly complicated to calculate, because in-house experiences and reference values from benchmarks are missing. The results have so far been disillusioning or even meaningless. But if you establish a DQ request database right from the start of a DQ project, after a certain initial period the benefits can be reported. Time and effort versus the potential harm of DQ defects may be estimated. With this information, for example, the size of the necessary DQ team can be determined.

That sounds great. But let's take a break and go for dinner. We will continue our conversation at the restaurant.

1.5   Requirements for Data Quality

As I understood your DQ definition, you first need to devise requirements for DQ, before you go about measuring it, no matter how you will accomplish that part. The terms DQ requirements, DQ criteria and DQ rules frequently appear in this context. For me, they sound quite alike. Could you please help me with a little private lesson, and I think I will take the sea bass - what about you?

DQ requirement is the generic term for expectations concerning the quality of a certain information object (e.g. database, table, data file, data selection, field). These quality expectations may be sub-divided into more general DQ criteria (like currency and completeness). Using object-specific and -appropriate DQ rules (so-called business rules), one can evaluate to which extent a criterion is met.

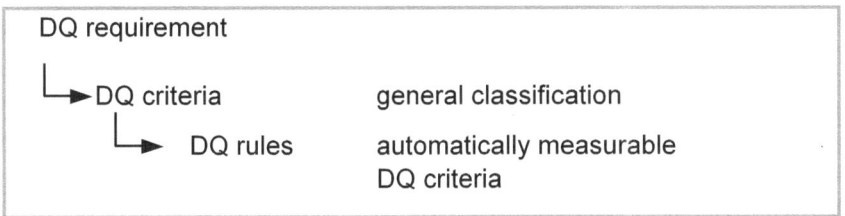

For DQ rules, as well as for DQ criteria, there are DQ goals, thresholds for a traffic light status, and weightings for the aggregation of results.

A DQ attribute refers either to an applied DQ rule or a DQ criterion.

Are all these differentiations really necessary?

Yes, at least if you have to handle a great number of DQ rules and if you wish to keep the DQ reports or the DQ statements in a more general mode. Proceeding in this way, it is possible, for example, to compare all checked results of several DQ rules concerning completeness, to aggregate them, and to make a general statement about completeness.

1.6   Data Quality Statements

What does a DQ statement look like?

DQ statements about a certain information object (specific data selection, data file, table, database) express, in percent, the degree to which pre-defined DQ requirements are met. For the correct evaluation of the computed percentage it is important to draw comparisons with determined reference values and earlier results, for instance:

1. Summary

Information object	Table 4711
Date	dd.mm.20yy
DQ index	85 %
DQ status	green
DQ tendency	ascending
DQ target	89 %
Previous results:	82 % (1 week ago)
	90 % (1 month ago)

Threshold values

Green	Yellow	Red
>= 85 %	>= 83 % and < 85 %	< 83%

2. Absolute values

Number of examined data records:	1.2 Mio.
Number of data records with DQ defects:	40,000
Number of critical DQ defects:	100,000

3. Detailed information

Here the results of the DQ check are listed on the level of DQ criteria and assigned DQ rules.

(1-n) DQ criterion, actual index, set target, status, weighting, previous results

   (1-n) DQ rule, actual index, set target, status, weighting, previous results

   If necessary drill-down to data defects

I have never seen a workout of DQ details like that in our company. But before getting any deeper into the act, would you please summarize the main statements I should keep in mind:

There is no DQ statement without DQ measurement; frankly speaking **"if you can't measure it, you can't manage it!"**[3]

Credibility, reliability and trustworthiness are the main arguments for the development of DQ statements.

Why is it that the market should have more confidence in us if we had DQ statements? Is that not just a typical flowery phrase of the consultancy club?

That certainly depends on the precise statement and on its basis. Maybe the following short episode from my everyday life as a DQ consultant will be helpful:

A manager asked me to illustrate DQ effects by means of a business report with some risk-relevant key figures, scaling to a two-digit billion Euro level. So I arbitrarily pointed at one of the key figures and asked how it is calculated. He explained a lot, but he was not able to find the documentation for this relevant and considerably high figure straight away. With a functioning DQ service for regulatory needs, the task would have been a child's play.

I continued to ask how he could be sure that the figure in question is correct. He reported that the figure is a sum from a reporting system and that it is compared with the addition of other subtotals

---

[3] This famous phrase is equally assigned to Peter F. Drucker, US-American economist, and to Robert S. Kaplan, inventor of the balanced scorecard.

from the transactional systems. If there are no discrepancies, the calculated sum is correct. With a sceptical smile on my face, I asked him if it ever happens that no discrepancy occurs, and if it does, is it being recorded? The manager explained that discrepancies are not allowed; therefore they perform data reconciliations as long as the discrepancies disappear. But there are no records about this procedure. I told the manager, if I were the auditor from the regulator, I would end the inspection at this point, get up and leave!

Only after I insisted further that there are always discrepancies between reporting and transactional systems did he acknowledge that recorded adjustment bookings have always been made and that these bookings can be as high as in the hundreds of millions.

Corrections are not revealed automatically, because otherwise, the quality of the core data might be doubted unnecessarily!

DQ index values inform about the quality of relevant key figures. The auditor would, for instance, easily recognise the completeness of our mentioned key figure, if the discrepancies in a comparison over all systems stayed below a previously defined threshold. He would be informed in detail how larger discrepancies are handled in the company. Furthermore, he would be able to view the results of each comparison in an illustrative table.

With access to DQ statements the manager in the delineated episode might not have had any distress in explaining matters; instead, he would have appeared more competent.

The catch phrases credibility, reliability and trustworthiness become more objective when supported by DQ results -- they are definitely not merely flowery consultant slogans.

*Okay, you convinced me. In our company there are comparable proced-
ures and it is desirable to increase objectivity.*

*Now let us take the next step and see which organisational requirements
have to be met to professionally run DQ. I would like to come back to the
DQ criteria.*

2 Organisational Requirements

Tell me: how many DQ criteria are we actually talking about?

2.1 DQ Criteria (7+2)

Some time ago, we encountered 45 DQ criteria. To us it seemed important to determine how they might be checked and we found the following six essential checking methods:

- Methods which should be covered by expert's approval (e.g. interpretability, granularity, necessity)
- Surveys (e.g. objectivity, relevance, intelligibility trustworthiness, added value)
- Methods covered by IT security /business monitoring (e.g. access opportunity, access security, temporary availability)
- Automatic measuring methods
- Methods requiring a visual inspection or a document check (traceability, normative consistency, origin)
- Methods comprising audits / follow-up examinations (e.g. applicability, applicability of audits)

We think it doesn't make sense to engage the DQ team in tasks that are already professionally handled by other teams in the company. Therefore the DQ criteria may in principle be confined to 7 automatically measurable criteria and two documentary criteria (7+2).

Table 1: DQ Criteria (7+2)

	DQ criteria[4]	Description
Automatically measurable	(1) Completeness per row (horizontal completeness)	Is there any missing or defective data in a record? All data is entered according to business needs.
	(2) Syntactical correctness (conformity)	Is there data in a non-standardised format? The data fits into the specific format.
	(3) Absence of contradictions (consistency)	Which data values are contradictory? The data do not contradict integrity specifications (business rules, empirical values) or defined ranges of values (within the data pool, in comparison with other data pools, in time elapsed).
	(4) Accuracy incl. currency	Which data is wrong or expired? Correct and up to date (timeliness) notation of existing names, addresses, products etc.
	(5) Absence of repetitions (free of duplicates)	Which data records or contents of columns are being repeated? No duplicates (search for synonyms and similarities), no homonyms, no overlapping (continuity), everything is precisely identifiable (uniqueness).
	(6) Business referential integrity (integrity)	Which reference data or relations are missing? There will not be any clients without a contract, products will be listed, ...
	(7) Completeness (Cross check sums, vertical completeness)	Is there data consistency over all systems? For instance: at an appointed date the number of contracts in the data source is exactly the same as the number of contracts in the DWH.

---

[4] DQ Criteria 1 through 7 correspond to the 7 Basic DQ Rule Types

Table 1: (continuation)

DQ criteria	Description
Documentary	(8) Availability of documenta-tion (findability)	Can the data be found easily and quickly (e.g. using common "search"-functions) Are the data tagged?
	(9) Normative consistency	It has to be assured that the naming and meaning of certain data is the same over all systems, processes and departments of the organisation.

Actually, in the course of an internal survey, I already came across 19 dimensions of DQ, but I like 7+2 a good deal more. Sometimes less is better, isn't it? However, from my staff I heard before that in matters of Solvency II just 3 DQ criteria are sufficient.

Indeed, in the context of Solvency II, only three DQ performance indicators are requested: appropriateness, accuracy and completeness of data. But when it came to the question of how these criteria should be checked, we had to fall back on the 7+2 criteria introduced above. In the meantime we are convinced that each DQ criterion comprising automatic and/or documentary components can be described with our 7+2 criteria. Let's take a look at the next figure.

Thank you so far. Thinking it over seriously, criterion no. 9 - "normative consistency" - is rather tricky. We will have to turn our company upside down if that actually needs to be achieved.

You've got it! ☺ No! Let's stay realistic; even for criterion 8, "availability of documentation", nobody being even a little familiar with actually running IT systems would ever expect that each data field is documented and traceable! However, in regard to economic key figures, only a single documentation – and not various – should exist, using the same labels across all sources. For example, if sales figures (field/column "fee") are aggregated from various business departments, it simply must not occur that data from department A includes insurance tax, while data from department B doesn't.

For the case that a central documentation of the most important data definitions of the company is aimed for, it would furthermore be reasonable that the system supports the departments in the course of harmonizing business terms (definitions). It is important to keep everything in a reasonable frame.

What about „technical correctness“ as a DQ criterion?

If you are referring to concepts like "correctness in regard to contents" or "absence of professional errors", I unfortunately have to disappoint you. This is one of the problems computers cannot solve[5]. As an alternative, you might try to define evaluable sub-aspects of "technical correctness" and test these sub-aspects, like actuality, completeness, valid syntax, absence of contradiction etc. On the level of single cases the sum of these sub-aspects might be sufficient to cover what is meant by "technical correctness". However, the isolated use of terms like "correctness", "correctness with regard to contents" and "technical correctness" in a DQ environment may be revealed as wishful thinking, or security strategies which DQ just cannot provide.

Two examples from day-to-day business:

(1) After bonuses for new customers are paid, some old customers are generated anew in the system with small modifications – for instance in name or address. DQ then detects that 75% of the data

---

[5] A topic in „theoretic computer science“, the so-called "halting problem" of the Turing machine, applied to correctness of data.

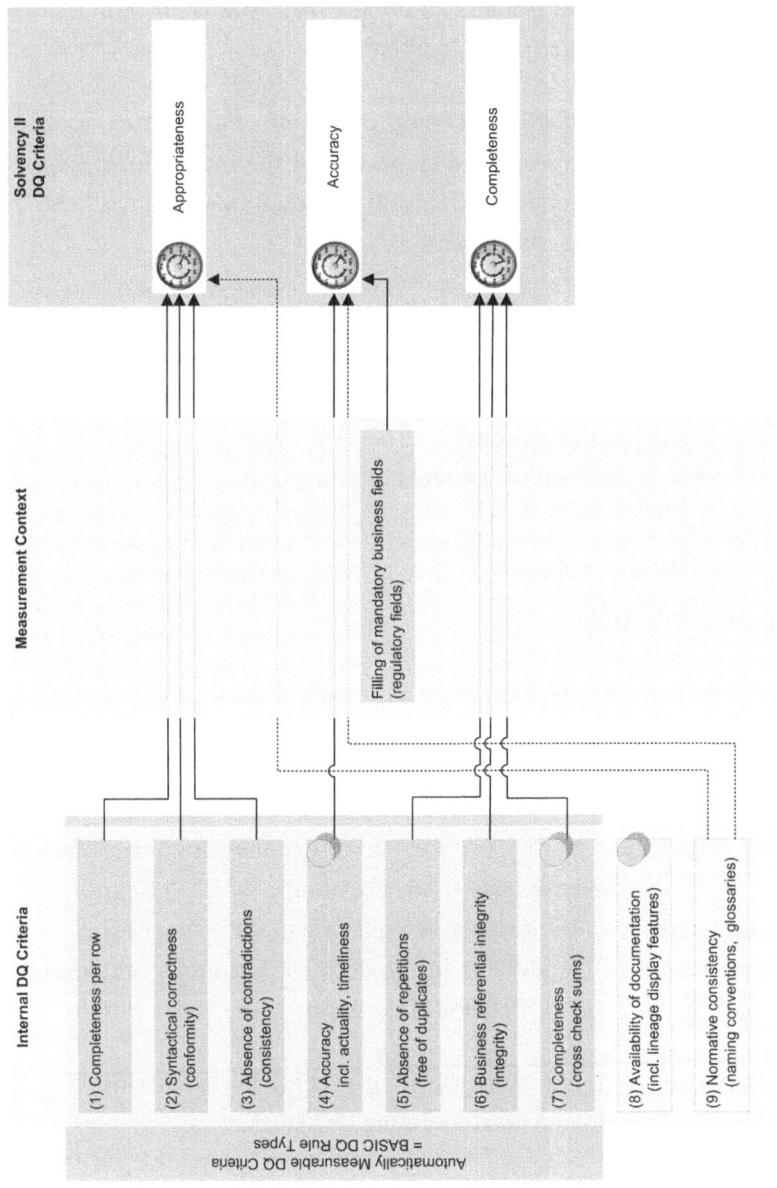

Figure 1: Mapping Internal DQ Criteria to SII DQ Criteria

of two customers are identical. The employee confirms that these actually are two customers and that everything is all right. Is that "correctness with regard to contents"?

(2) By the end of the year, in some companies the contract applications regularly increase and at the end of the first following quarter they are cancelled without any interaction with the client. Is that "professional correctness"?

I hope these examples illustrate the limitations of DQ. It is not an objective of DQ to serve this kind of investigative purpose. It's up to the particular employees responsible for the data (data owner) and other services to provide professional and content correctness, meaning that the data gives an account of the real conditions.

Examples for DQ Rules

Please give me some examples for automatically measurable DQ criteria, so things become clearer! Shall we order some more wine?

Sure, no problem. But you should keep in mind, even if the arbitrary naming of DQ rules might have a trivial touch, they are only definable after a thorough data analysis (data profiling), which has to be conducted together with the respective data users/ data owner. This guarantees that later on DQ defects in the defined data areas can be automatically detected, quantified and if necessary corrected.

A possible relief: If the data profiling repeatedly reveals no critical abnormalities, there is no need to define DQ rules.

Example (1) Completeness per row (horizontal completeness)

Rule „customer record for automobile insurance": Here it is verified that all fields which are minimally needed for creating a customer record for the automobile insurance are actually filled in. If more than 5% of the data do not reach the criterion, the responsible department is informed.

Rule „not empty for regulator authorities": It is checked that previously defined data fields are not empty before being further processed. All data sets failing this criterion are immediately handed over to the responsible employee in an adequate way.

Example (2) Syntactic correctness (conformity)

Rule „format gender": In a selected data pool the following labels are accepted: m, f, male, female, masculine, feminine, homen, mulher, hermaphrodite, fm: formerly man, fm: formerly woman. Empty or differently completed data sets have to be marked for an immediate correction.

Rule „format date": Data in the fields A, C, E are permitted only in one of the following patterns dd.mm.yy, ddmmyy and mm/dd/yyyy. Any other pattern will cause problems in further computations. Incorrect data sets are rejected and handed over to the responsible employee.

Example (3) Absence of contradictions (consistency)

Rule „gender and title": Despite all implemented plausibility checks, sometimes the data is partly contradictory. In such a case it is checked whether title and gender are contradictory.

Rule „premium smaller than amount insured": A violation of

this rule sometimes occurs when a new product has been introduced and if there are reasons to not implement such a plausibility check in the near future.

Example (4) Accuracy including currency

Rule „actuality of the business report": The business report compares actual data with data dating back up to four years. A report is up to date if at least 20 to 30 % of the data sets have a time signature from the past twelve months.

Rule „actual portfolio": The register does neither include only formerly distributed nor future products („valid until" <today, „valid from">today).

Example (5) Absence of repetitions (free of duplicates)

Rule „unique annual premium": The combination of the fields "number of contract", "year" and "amount" may only appear once in table x.

Rule „unique customer": There may not be two or more data records in which the following data fields show similarities of more than 95 %.

Example (6) Business referential integrity (integrity)

Rule „only known processing indicators (KPI)": No data will be transferred if their KPI is missing in the table of "List of workable KPI in the DWH".

Rule „no fakes": There will be no insurance application with a product name, which is not listed, in the "actual portfolio".

Example (7) Completeness (cross check sums)

> Rule „completeness of reserves": The difference between sum
> x and number y is always bigger than 0 and the difference for
> the instance should not exceed 0,01 % in a report period.

> Rule „sales figures": The difference between the sum of the
> sales figures and the number Y from DWH may not exceed
> 0,3%. If so, department XYZ has to be informed immediately.

That's it!

Thanks for the material. However, I can imagine that most of your exam-
ples are already taken account of in our company.

As I conceded initially, I believe that the lion's share of the cases described is already taken care of. But from active DQ projects I learned
that there is hardly ever a stringent system or a protocol on the results
of DQ tests. We frequently encounter confusions with protocols from
job control and ETL. They usually inform us only about aborts in the
processing, why they happened (DQ deficits maybe a trigger) and how
much data has been processed.

How can you be sure that DQ does not serve as a disguise for the new
development of lots of applications just for testing purposes if other pro-
grams are running correctly?

Yes, and in a little while even more new programmes will appear in
the market to check whether everything was correct in past DQ tests.
And over all checks and crosschecks we will forget that the company
has more substantive things to accomplish and louse up business in
spite of the best possible DQ.

Sorry for being sarcastic, but somehow, you are right. There actually is this hazard. Besides all efforts to do things right, the objective of DQ has to be kept in mind! Which is to detect errors in the data and taken as a whole to make data more reliable. DQ cannot serve as test- or acceptance-authority for already implemented or new programmes, since that would really mean doing the same thing twice over. But we can utilize DQ in a highly meaningful way for measurements before and after migrations with consistent criteria. However, if defects are discovered, it is not always possible to attribute them to bugs in the new programme or to handling problems.

Okay, we had better leave the further discussion to the experts. But may I ask for a short explanation of the differences between data profiling and DQ rules!

Of course! Let's try to do that with the help of the previously intro-duced analogy of water quality. We consider data profiling as a kind of "global analysis of water quality", where analytical chemists do not yet know what they are looking for. They apply some standard pro-cedures, for example the search for the number of germs (in the case of data we would speak about column analysis). Because of earlier in-cidences the chemists already have reasonable suspicions. As soon as the disturbing contaminations are identified, the critical spots will be equipped with a simple monitoring device. For instance a small box with pH value monitor, contrast agent and scale. Depending on the water source or position, there are several individual options to keep the pH value within a certain range. Swinging back to DQ: DQ rules serve as a simple monitoring mechanism and if necessary, DQ deals with certain defects.

I think we have had enough DQ for today. Let's drop the subject and close with the following thought:

With a DQ System you surely cannot prevent people from making mistakes. But in principle, data defects can be detected earlier, especially those that occur with certain regularity. And they can be eliminated with comparatively little time and effort.

After some time filled with small talk about other matters, the two friends say goodbye and agree to meet again, when they will mainly concentrate on the embedding of DQ within the organisation.

At the Following Meeting

In the meantime I could not get DQ out of my mind. What I am missing, however, is a concrete idea about how everything is supposed to run and what a DQ specialist is going to do all day long.

You will surely have a better picture in a few minutes. Let us first discuss the necessary operational roles. As soon as we continue with the DQ main processes, we will have a better basis for addressing the issue of the DQ specialist's tasks. From my point of view we have to deal with three essential organisational aspects:

- operational roles,
- expected results and how they should be achieved (DQ main processes),
- continuous workflow, including its perpetuation as well as accessibility of all essential departments of the company (build-up organisation).

I'm curious about it!

2.2 Operational DQ Roles

It makes sense to delegate this new, complex and very sensitive topic to only a few, excellently trained employees, forming a DQ Team.

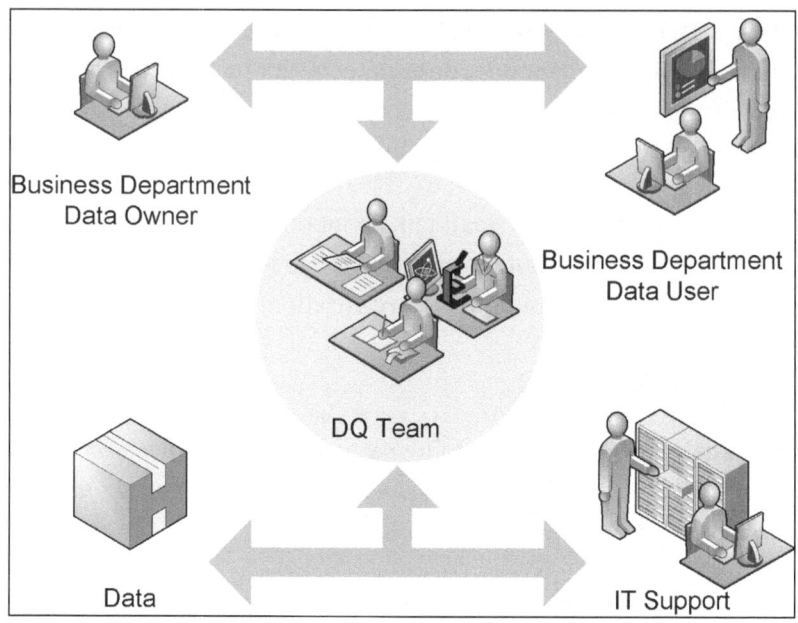

Figure 2:   DQ operational roles

Actually I thought DQ concerns everyone and is not restricted to just a few employees.

Quite right. The members of the DQ team (furthermore they will also be referred to as DQ specialists) cannot take over responsibility for the quality of the other employees' data. But they can provide detailed reports about the quality of the data to those responsible, and can help to identify critical DQ defects across departments.

That sounds as if the team might be compared to some kind of technical data control board?

Exactly! We consider the DQ team as a service provider for the specific departments including IT, especially for migration projects. The departments and IT can request certain services, so they do not need their own expensive DQ tools and DQ specialists. Moreover, the DQ team will serve as drop-in centre within the company, which neutrally performs all DQ measurements for critical business data and key figures.

Will the DQ team be aligned functionally or rather technically?

Both. The ideal candidate for a DQ team comes with pronounced analytic and good IT skills (for instance to carry out data base queries), quickly grasps specific data-related topics, and is able to work equally well in methodological and pragmatic ways. When a DQ team takes up work, they will initially focus on the new techniques (DQ tools, data requests, integration with ETL routines, etc.) and later, as soon as these techniques have become more or less routine, the business aspect will dominate.

Where is the ideal location for a DQ team?

For companies with systemic relevance in their countries – and these are the ones the financial regulators will have a special eye on – I would suggest a strictly functional separation. This means that the DQ team carrying out the DQ measurements should neither be responsible for data care, data transport, data transformation or data refinement. Just like a technical data control board! The DQ team reports, consults and accompanies. As a rule it should not execute any operational actions.

Where a DQ team actually is located does not matter at all! It should be placed where potential conflicts of interest are minimal and undisturbed open communication is possible.

Summary:

DQ team

As a neutral entity the DQ team informs about data quality in a company, turns DQ requests into measurable figures, reports about all DQ measures, and advises the responsible data owners with respect to feasible DQ improvements, but the team itself does not have any responsibility for the data.

Apart from the DQ team which other roles are to be considered?

There are three other roles:

Data owner

He or she is the professional responsible for certain applications and data areas, data access, and the functional correctness of data as well as for their collection and care. He or she defines DQ goals and monitors them with the support of the DQ team.

Data user

To do her job she needs data from others and formulates expectations regarding the quality of these data.

IT-/technical application supporter

He gives support if technical questions arise, concerning applications and their data. He is the only technical contact person for the DQ team for the particular application/function. He either belongs to the staff of the IT department or he is an application developer from the business department. In rather exceptional cases, an employee of the Electronic Data Processing Center might also be the technical contact person.

How about responsibilities? Does the data owner continue to be responsible for his data, even if it is received and further processed by others?

A data owner is answerable for data quality as agreed upon only to his direct data customers (data users). A person or group is classified as data user while acting in the role of a "familiar" recipient of data. As soon as data users take over data in order to process or to distribute it, they become the new data owners. And now they are responsible for the quality of these data for any further recipient.

Why do you emphasize the recipient as a "familiar recipient"?

DQ is directly linked with the purpose of use. A data owner cannot be held responsible for data, which an unknown data user utilizes for unknown purposes. In such cases he cannot promise a quality level or give any other guarantees.

There is a parallel to process responsibility, isn't it?

As right as rain! The persons responsible for processes or parts of processes are in principle our data owners. They request DQ standards from their data providers and give DQ guaranties to their data recipients. But let us return to this topic later, when we have reached a better understanding of DQ.

So, you get along with the four roles outlined above?

For the description of the DQ main processes it is sufficient to know these four roles and their interaction. That facilitates a clear view. Particularly since it is irrelevant if in certain situations the data owner is substituted by a local DQ representative or whether a DQ team consists of DQ managers and DQ specialists (several further roles will be presented later).

Which are the DQ main processes?

2.3   DQ Processes

To begin with, we know the DQ process (DQ-P) as a general data quality process with the aim to increase the average DQ level. Since the financial regulators request statements about the DQ of economic risk figures and other critical concerned figures (Solvency), we modelled another DQ main process and refer to it as DQ-R, meaning data quality for regulatory needs. The primary task of DQ-R is to produce DQ statements for any critical concerned figure along the data origin pathway.

2.3.1   General Data Quality Process (DQ-P)

At this point we will illustrate the single steps of a DQ check request. The result/target of this process is to increase data quality, including detailed DQ statements about the appearance of certain DQ defects within a defined data area. The process represents the general DQ processing situation and is normally used as a reference model.

The core process of DQ-P is geared to the five steps of the DQ measurement cycle.

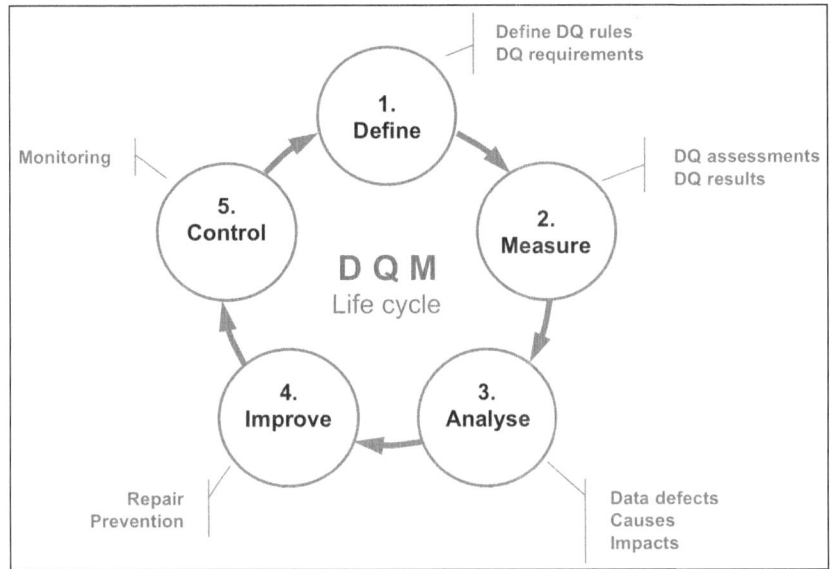

Figure 3:   DQM Life cycle

The process starts with the acceptance of the DQ request (identification).

Usually existing infrastructure and organisational requirements call for an adaptation of the process.

In the following, a short example of the DQM core process (see figure 7 in appendix)[6]:

---

[6] Further information and diagrams are also available under „CC DQM" at www.morbey.de.

Step 0: Registration of a DQ request or a DQ incident

The DQ team starts its activities with the acceptance of the request for a DQ check. Normally, the request comes from the data owner or data user (also from IT in case of migration projects).

The DQ team enters the DQ request into a specific DQ request database, which facilitates the DQ job control and the reporting ability of the team. Afterwards the responsible IT supporter is asked to provide at least read access to the data and the corresponding data documentation ("provide data").

Steps 1, 2 and 3: Define, Measure and Analyse

These work steps are arranged in a loop. At the first contact with new data, the DQ specialist regularly starts a data profiling. For example, an automatic column analysis will be made. The DQ specialist tries to gain first insights into the data from the statistical analysis (pattern, frequency distribution, etc.). Thereafter, a clarification with the data owner will follow, and if necessary with the IT supporter or the data user (assistance, adjustment).

Insights from data profiling are used to define the data quality rules for specific DQ criteria (second step in iteration). By applying the DQ rules it will be possible for the first time to measure data quality. After the new data analysis and evaluation of the DQ measurement results, the last iteration step will be at issue: definition of DQ goals together with the data owner/data users.

The result will be an official data quality check routine – established by the DQ team - which can be applied at any time to measure the data quality of the concerned data (DQ repeated check). Now data quality defects can be identified and evaluated; and, if needed, further actions can be initiated. The results of official DQ checks will be saved in a standard format and made available for further examination.

Steps 4 and 5: Improve and Control

After the previous steps, we will be able to issue DQ statements. And then? It will be generally up to the data owner, to initiate further activities. The DQ team supports him in the conceptual design of measures and in determining possible alternatives to improve data quality and to prevent the recurrence of already identified DQ defects.

The most effective prevention method is the installation of another plausibility check close to the origin of the defects, in order to rule out storage and further processing of deficient data. On behalf of the data owner IT will arrange that.

If occasionally it's not possible to follow that path – which might actually happen – there are at least two DQ operations to handle the problem: DQ monitoring and DQ controlling.

The DQ check routines, previously established by the DQ team, will, for example, be embedded in the data delivery paths. Each record with identified DQ defects is marked and logged (DQ monitoring). It will be sufficient to inform the data owner, if ex post data corrections neither strain people nor systems.

In the case that subsequent systems request a high quality of the incoming data, DQ Controlling springs into action. Data with critical or suspicious defects are rejected. They are either directly send back to the Data Owner or intermediately parked. Under no circumstances are they processed further as though they were correct! Parked data is checked and afterwards approved or sent back to the data owner. Supported by the DQ team the IT department (usually an ETL programmer) implements DQ controlling stations, utilising DQ tools.

In this phase, the DQ team provides the data owner with first concepts, decision backgrounds and DQ reports and accompanies him during the implementation of improvement measures.

I call these 5 steps the basics for each DQ specialist. And I hope that my excursion answers your question concerning the DQ specialist's duties.

By the way, just like in waterworks alongside the water pipes, a network of DQ measurement and control points will arise by and by along the information flow, securing high data quality (see Figure 4). And there will be regular reports on the actually encountered data quality.

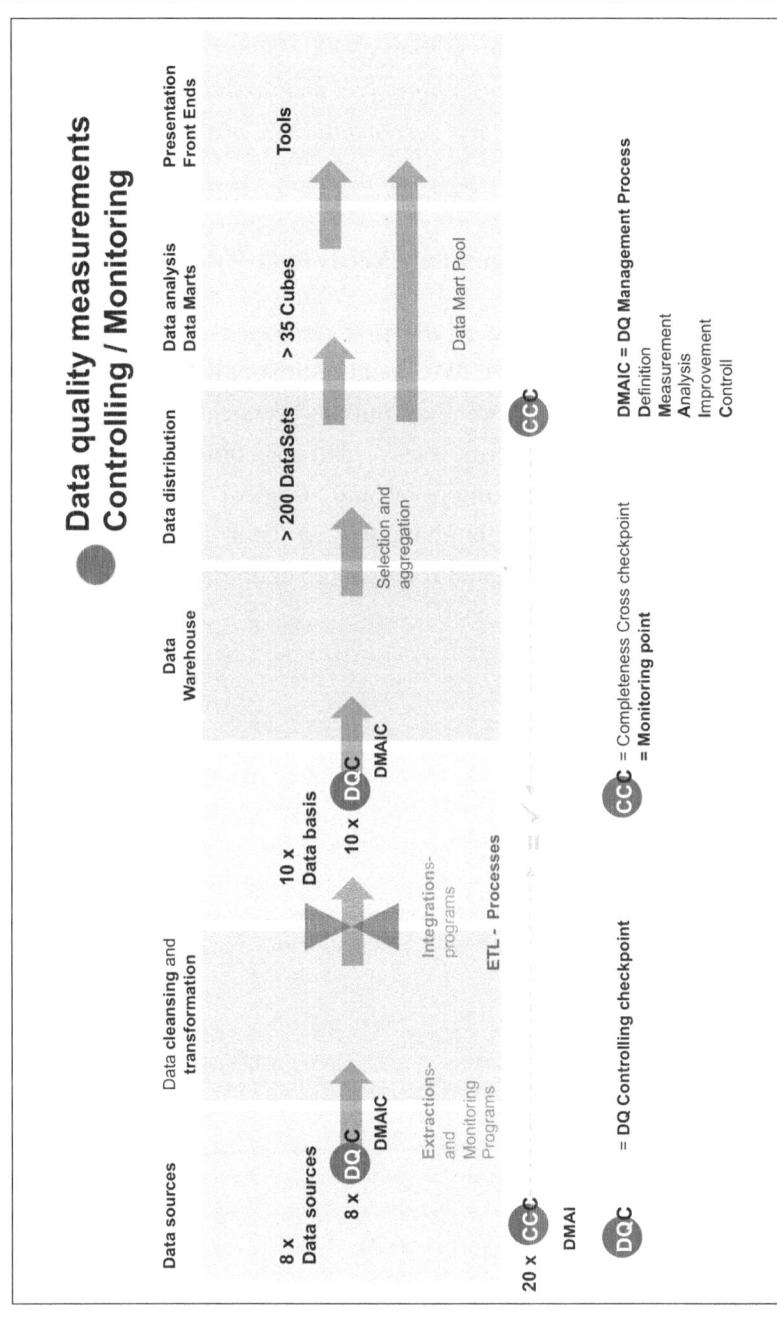

Figure 4: Example of data pathways with DQ checkpoints

Well, thank you, now things are getting clearer. Beyond dispute these are reasonable activities. In the beginning, you mentioned DQ-R. So I guess, DQ specialists have some more responsibilities besides those already mentioned.

2.3.2   Data Quality for Regulatory Needs (DQ-R)

Quite right. In comparison to the first described process, DQ-R appears to some extent easier. We could almost call it "DQ light", because in step 2 "Define" we may initially concentrate on fewer key aspects like "vertical completeness" and "accuracy including actuality". The last two steps "Improve" and "Control" are not always obligatory. However, DQ-R is characterized by a documentary focus, which is not usually trivial and requires the cooperation of IT, the data owner and the DQ team.

Table 2: Descriptive elements of an information object
in a meta database

Descriptive elements of an information object (data, tables, fields etc.)	Involvement		
	IT	Business	DQ team
1 Business description (semantics) Relation to glossary		X	
2 Technical description Structural description Syntax and value range ...	X		
3 Origin of information (incl. transformation rules) Maintenance of relationships	X		
4 Organisational allocation Data owner IT supporter ...	X	X	+
5 DQ requirements DQ rules DQ checkpoint		+	X

According to the available infrastructure and documentation, the process has to be adapted in such a way that the responsible employee can access following information if DQ-related questions arise:

- Actual data lineages for any business-critical key figures (complete information flow mapping of a key figure back to its sources in the production systems, displaying intermediate data, steps of transformation and organisational responsibilities),
- DQ checkpoints along the lineages,

- Test object, test rules plus test cycle at every DQ checkpoint,
- DQ check results in their chronological variation at every DQ checkpoint (going back 12 months, i.e. use test).

2.4   Operating Expense

How about the operating expense for the two processes?

After the description of the DQ-R process, the initial size of the DQ team, the duration of the first activities as well as the surplus load on business and IT will be easily estimated with the help of our extrapolation model.

As to DQ-P we will have reliable estimations only after an initial period, on the basis of completed DQ requests.

Well then, let's start with the DQ-R process and postpone DQ-P.

At first glance, that would be a good approach. But it doesn't make any sense to leave identified critical DQ defects within the system. So, the DQ team will initially spend at least 20% of the available budget on the support of the general DQ-P (that is to say from the entire DQ budget approximately 20% will have to be allotted to DQ-P and 80% to DQ-R).

An example:

A company has to audit about 50 business-critical key figures on process security. There are 14 relevant applications with 12 interfaces, which will result in approximately 200 DQ check requests.

Assuming a DQ team of 4 employees, 2.7 employees will be exclusively busy fulfilling these requests for about 13 months. Then all DQ-R requests will be handled once. Business and IT will regularly provide about 0.7 or 1.1 project days (PD) per DQ-R request (incl. training and audits).

The remaining 1.3 DQ specialists will be concerned with the running DQ service. This suggests that during the first year the DQ team will have about 90 PD for the support of DQ-P at their disposal and circa 50 PD for DQ consulting, DQ monitoring and administration. As already mentioned, the necessary operating expenses of business and IT cannot be estimated yet.

As soon as all necessary DQ statements have been generated initially, the proportions in the annual DQ budget will almost completely turn around to 85 % for DQ-P and 15 % for DQ-R.

Which experiences are there in regard to the size of DQ teams?

The size surely depends on the additional results, which will be expected of the DQ team. In the long run it seems realistic that the number of DQ specialists exclusively tied up with DQ duties should range between 1 and 2 % of those employed in IT.

During the starting period, that is to say until all DQ-R requests are completed and the main requirements for DQ-P are satisfied, the above given estimation has to be doubled. The starting phase can extent over 1.5 to 3.5 years, depending on the complexity and condition of a company's data.

Our experience teaches that a DQ Team should comprise at least 3 full-time DQ specialists at the outset.

It is getting clearer and clearer to me, that DQ is a serious topic with tremendous impact. And that's why I will need a good manager, who knows how to contain costs.

A goal-oriented and pragmatic DQ manager would be a good choice, for sure. The great magic trick will be to focus on the critical values and work with a small range of adequately placed DQ checkpoints in the most important data pathways. Although a one hundred percent DQ coverage of all points is desirable, the actual implementation may turn out to have its difficulties. A balance between operating effort and the benefit of DQ has to be maintained in an adequate relation to the company's business objective.

2.5   Organisational Structure

Let's assume there is a DQ team comprising a DQ manager and several DQ specialists that works on request. But how does it receive DQ requests?

It is extremely important that the management board requests data quality statements from the DQ responsible person of each business unit. They are going to approach the particular data owners in their department and they in turn will ask the DQ team for support.

The elaboration of DQ statements applying DQ-R will make up to 80 % of the initial tasks of a DQ team.

Data users and data owners who identify disturbing DQ defects, will address IT or the DQ team either directly or via helpdesk. These requests will be worked off according to DQ-P. In the beginning, this kind of activity will add up to only about 20 % of the total amount of work.

If the management board signals hardly any interest in DQ statements, it is obvious that it will take substantively more time to install a DQ service.

You already mentioned several roles for staff members. Which other roles will have a serious part in the DQ organisation?

Besides the already outlined roles, DQ does not require any significant new roles. I brought a governance model with me, which may serve as guideline for an effective DQ organisation.

The whole purpose of a DQ governance model is to emphasise authority, in order to guarantee a smooth functioning of all DQ-associated processes.

DQ representative per legal entity

> The DQ representative is a member of the management board and is responsible for the entire company's data quality and data security.

DQ representative per business unit

> Has to provide DQ statements for all business-relevant data areas under his responsibility. Requests DQ goals and DQ reports for his unit and authorizes the budget for DQ improvements and business data documentation.

Head of IT (systems + applications environment)

> Is responsible for the technical infrastructure and the safe working of applications and systems. Provides the necessary IT resources and requests DQ statements, especially for migration projects.

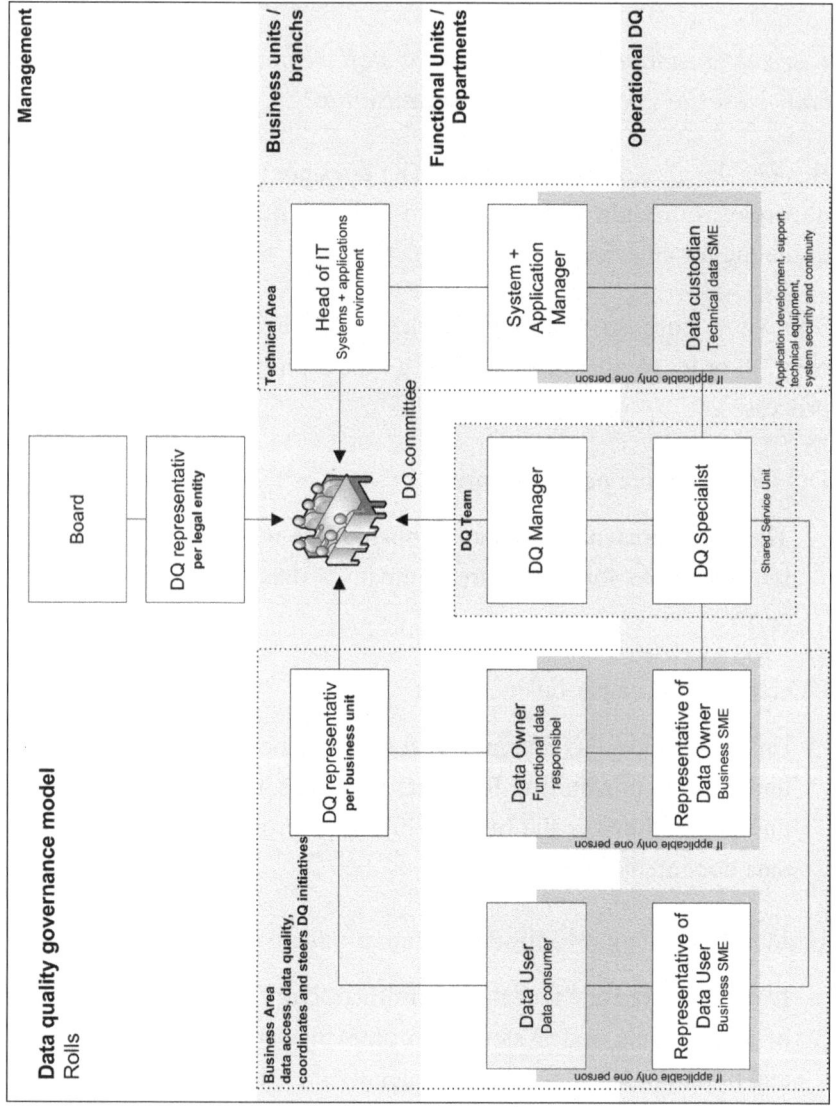

Figure 5: Data quality governance model

DQ manager

Is head of the DQ team and manages the DQ requests. At regular intervals he publishes DQ reports on business critical data areas.

DQ committee

Is the superior DQ governance instance, headed by the company DQ representative.

The DQ committee sets up and approves the framework for the company-wide DQ strategy. For example: check requests for certain areas are issued and agreements on the focus of the DQ check criteria for Solvency II are brought about.

Representative of Data User/Data Owner
Local DQ representative

He signs and is responsible for the coordination and steering of DQ activities in the business departments and might serve as a speaker for several data users and data owners; indeed, he himself can be a data user or data owner. It is among the duties of each department to assign the specific roles and persons represent the department in matters of DQ measurement and reporting. Please assign this role to a business data subject matter expert (Business SME).

System / application manager

He is responsible for the currency of the technical data documentation, for integrity, accessibility, authenticity and confidentiality of the data. He supports the integration of DQ monitoring, respectively DQ controlling mechanisms into the application landscape. He may be identical with the data custodian / technical data SME.

DQ specialist

> Works in the DQ team, handles DQ check requests, accompanies
> DQ improvement measures and attends to the centrally provided
> DQ information networks.

*The DQ committee sounds good. But who is going to set it up, in which
intervals will it meet and how will the outcomes of these meetings be reported? Could you please say something about these issues?*

It is a typical responsibility of the DQ manager to prepare such meetings. Here is an outline of a DQ report, which might lead to a struc-
tured and productive cooperation between all participants:

Structural model of a DQ report

1. **Status according to analyses from the DQ orders database**

   1.1. Regulatory requests (DQ-R requests)

   - Percentage and
   - Number of completed requests
   - Critical findings
   - Next steps (planning)

   1.2. General DQ (DQ-P requests)

   - Number of completed, current and open requests (in the order of criticality per report period)
   - Number of notifications / DQ defects per application/interface in report period
   - Estimation of the operating expenses versus prevented potential loss (impact)

2. **DQ Indices per application respectively by department + number of critical DQ defects in period**

Stage I	First year: Information for data owner Some examples of DQ dashboards per table / file
Stage II	Second year: Information for organisational line managers Some examples of DQ indices per file
Stage III	Third Year: Information for management DQ index per application / department
Stage IV	Fourth Year: If applicable, DQ index per legal entity

---

The stage-wise aggregation of the DQ information in the second part results from the availability of the data to be elaborated and the complexity of the composition of the information. The latter can be

framed in a simpler way and even more effectively after the execution
of many DQ-R requests and with the assistance of then available DQ
analyses.

*Now that's enough regarding organisational matters. Let's envisage the
technical requirements for our next meeting. I'm going to invite a colleague from our IT department, whom you should already know very
well. On that occasion I also hope to hear more about the things we
should pay special attention to during the initial phase.*

*Just let me shortly recap a couple of points which became clearer to me
today:*

**DQ statements will be requested from company's DQ
representatives.**

**The DQ team will be a service unit which works out DQ
statements for the data owners and data users.**

The DQ team has to rely on cooperation with Business and IT.

**After the goals for the DQ team are explicitly set, the process of
delivering results should be described and agreed without delays.**

3 Technical Requirements

At the next and provisionally last scheduled meeting, a few of the previous topics are summed up, in order to brief the colleague from IT. The atmosphere remains very familiar; all know each other for years. The participants from the customer side will not be further differentiated in the following section.

In the course of our last conversation you already mentioned a set of tools, which are obviously needed by the DQ team. Which are they in particular?

For a start we will need two to four software tools.

- A DQ tool for the DQ specialists, for fast analysis and quality measurement of the data.

- A meta database for the business, IT and DQ team, serving as the central storage of business and technical descriptions for regulatory relevant data. Among other things, this will allow for documentary retracing of data fields over all systems[7].

- A DQ request database utilized by the DQ team for the systematic collection and efficient processing of DQ check requests.

How do you want us to understand "for a start"; are there even more software tools necessary later on?

Sure, some more things are needed, but usually they already exist in a company's infrastructure, for example database staging areas, read ac-

---

[7] Data lineage analysis

cess to particular production data and, for later on, analysing options in the DWH for the producing suitable DQ reports to management on an application-/unit level (DQ control status).

3.1   DQ Tool

Can we get along without a DQ tool or how about developing our own?

DQ tools consist of two combinable components. One is directed to the initial data analysis (data profiling), while the second takes over the definition and analysis of DQ rules (data quality).

Data profiling provides heuristic analysis of so far unknown data. It enables DQ specialists to detect data patterns, that is, potential relations between columns, intersections between different tables, and so on. Only this initial familiarisation with the data allows the formulation of concrete DQ goals including thresholds.

With the formulation of DQ rules (business rules), DQ check routines are determined on a business level, mostly without programming. After this step, DQ will actually be measurable. DQ check routines should be usable/reusable by the business and IT at any time.

Results from repeated DQ check routines will be the basis for long-term statements on DQ.

Time and effort for DQ analysis without professional tools is commonly estimated to be five times higher than our actual calculation. Without a DQ tool the data would have to be analysed by personal interpretation, visual screening of columns in tables and without making use of statistical routines. DQ rules would have to be programmed in Access or SQL and the storage of DQ check results would have to be organised in a standard format for later analysis. The error rate, as well as project duration and expenses, would go up significantly.

Occasionally we face one or the other companies' claim of having a well functioning DQ service without particular DQ tools. Unfortunately, up till now I never had the opportunity to take a closer look at such a company. But I assume that they are among the DQ pioneers (launching out around 2001-2004) and that they invested a lot in own developments of DQ check processes/routines.

If we don't develop the tools by ourselves, is there anything that requires special attention?

I am not sure whether to label the following two important functionalities as "special", but they immediately came to mind:

- An uncomplicated integration of DQ check routines (as defined by data owners and DQ team) into the already existing data supply procedures. If that's possible, it would not take much effort to add DQ monitoring and, if necessary, DQ controlling.

- The option to easily use DQ scorecards per table/file right from the start. That would increase the initial acceptance by data owners / data users and their superiors.

3.2   Meta Database

Which is the immediate influence a metadata base exerts on measurable DQ?

There is no immediate and explicit relationship between the existence of a well-maintained meta database and measurable DQ.

Then why should it be necessary?

The meta database is a central tool for documentation and communication for business units, IT and the DQ team.

It facilitates, for example, the mapping of lineages, meaning documentary audit trails of any business-relevant key figures back to the input fields via different technical platforms. This is a central requirement of financial regulators in regard to data documentation.

Additionally a meta database should offer the identification of DQ check points along the lineages (up to the stepwise mapping of the entire DQ network) as well as the attribution of contact persons for each information object.

The following table illustrates the structure of descriptive elements of an information object.

Quite apart from the demands of the financial regulators you will have to take measures to fulfil DQ criteria nr. 8 "Availability of documentation" and nr. 9 "Normative consistency".

A well-maintained meta database will by and by implicitly make a significant contribution to DQ.

Table 2: Descriptive elements of an information object
in a meta database

Descriptive elements of an information object (data, tables, fields etc.)	Involvement		
	IT	Business	DQ team
1 Business description (semantics) Relation to glossary		×	
2 Technical description Structural description Syntax and value range ...	×		
3 Origin of information (incl. transformation rules) Maintenance of relationships	×		
4 Organisational allocation Data owner IT supporter ...	×	×	✛
5 DQ requirements DQ rules DQ checkpoint		✛	×

We have already invest quite a lot in the documentation of systems. Most of the things you addressed should be available in our company.

What you say is completely consistent with our experiences. In most cases, there are business and technical descriptions of the data (tables and fields), which can be made available by the responsible employees. But it also is a fact that the information is not centrally concentrated and enriched with references to business glossaries, transformation steps, responsibility areas, lineages and results of DQ analysis. That hampers access and turns it into a highly time-consuming matter.

Without a meta data base, maintaining the documentation of data relevant for financial regulators, including data relations as well as the analysis of the required lineages, is extremely time- and cost-consuming. I would even state that it is organisationally impracticable and unacceptable for the employees.

As far as I know, our IT already uses meta databases.

In application development there are several data dictionaries in use nowadays. But they are customised exclusively for IT purposes and can be operated only by IT specialists. It would have to be tested, whether they might be upgraded to meet the above-mentioned criteria.

Couldn't we alternatively develop such a database with our own resources?

In that case, you should plan for at least 200 project days and a 3 months lasting development time.

Which things should we specifically pay attention to?

Four essential aspects immediately occur to me:

- Interfaces to the import of available information, in order to avoid - re-entering   the documentation (structure descriptions of tables, files etc.).

- An intuitive user interface for business departments.

- Easy manual maintenance of information objects without too complex import interfaces (e.g. transformation steps between two or more files).

- Availability of automatic processes for the refresh of basic data (structure descriptions of tables and files).

3.3   DQ Request Database

Would it be practicable to adjoin a DQ request database at a future date?

No, it is important to use it right from the start. For it is a crucial success factor in a DQ project that the DQ team is able to report right from the first hour. As a pre-condition we need the central DQ request database, maintained by the DQ team. Other users will have access to it and they can at any time check the actual status of DQ requests and DQ improvements.

Moreover, the request database enables the DQ manager to carry out evaluations concerning the most frequent DQ defects, causes and impacts, as well as to actual and further expenses, amongst others for DQ improvements.

An export-interface to Excel would be sufficient. Any further analysis could be conducted there utilizing pivot procedures.

We hold a ticketing or rather an error notification system. Isn't it more than enough?

That should not constrain us. We already mapped the requirements mentioned above in a ticketing system and also realised them as a "stand alone". It did not take more than 20 project days.

It is simply important that such a system is available right from the start without wasting time on Excel data collection sheets or the like.

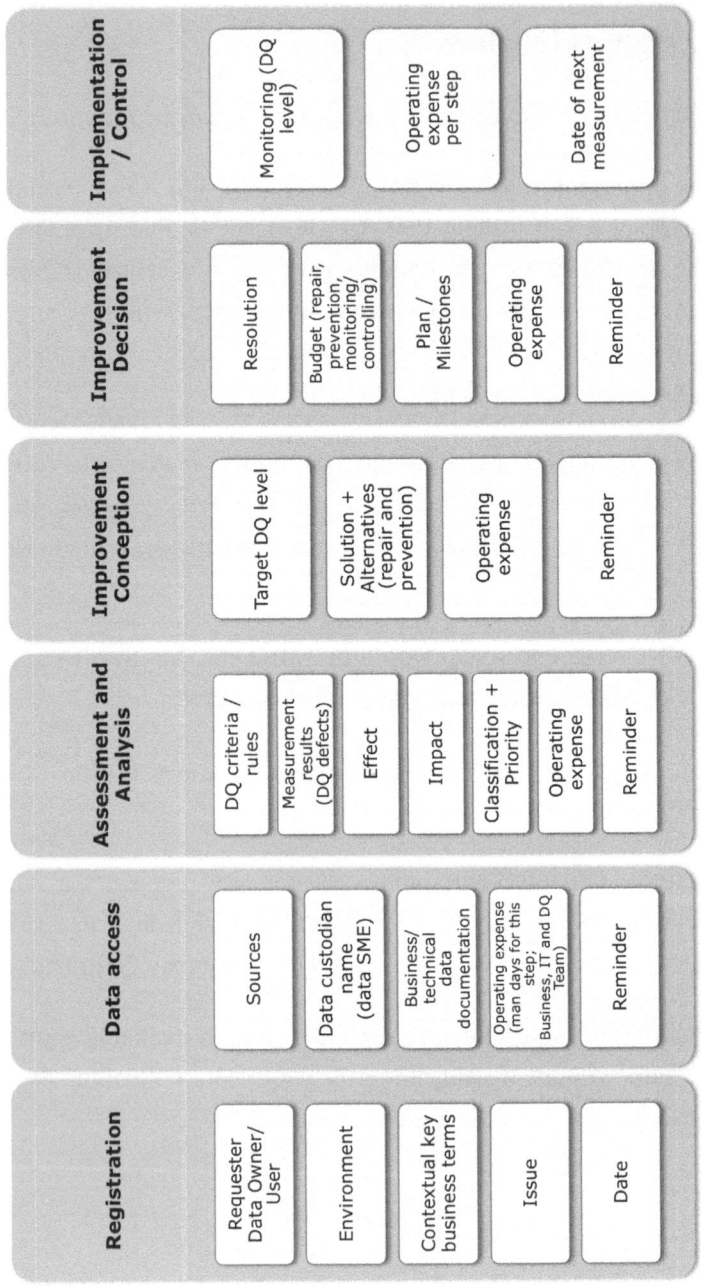

Figure 6: Elements of a DQ request in the DQ request database

4 Stumbling blocks

4.1 Initial Obstacles

Up to this point your explanations appear very comprehensible and well elaborated. So why is the topic of data quality so difficult to convey?

You yourself had a variety of questions that are not so easy to explain in a standard slide presentation, and you had to exercise some patience to get acquainted with the concept. The difficulties you address arise from four essential factors:

- challenging organisational allocation,

- misunderstanding of DQ,

- low awareness of the problem and

- not understanding the benefits.

4.1.1 Challenging organisational allocation

DQ is an infrastructure issue and situated exactly between business and IT. This means it cannot be clearly allocated, and consequently it is easily shuffled from one's responsibility to the others'. It is aggravating and possibly difficult having to deal with this additional duty. Furthermore DQ does not immediately result in higher sales and better acceptance by the markets. If a company is not actually struggling with DQ defects and regulatory demands for DQ statements have not yet to be met, the topic is consequently postponed.

4.1.2   Misunderstanding of DQ

As soon as you take a closer look at DQ, you will notice that apparently a lot of activities in the intended direction are already under way. Short of a deeper understanding, everything concerning data is rapidly subsumed under the rubric DQ (for instance data modelling, data organisation, data documentation, ETL programming and process security). The composition of a couple of risk figures in a DWH is taken for a DQ monitor. Some renowned consultancies try to promote DWH process audits and DHW process improvements as DQ management. And finally, I personally had the experience that ETL and job controlling protocols were praised as "DQ results".

Listening to all that, you might believe that enough is done already. Why should it be necessary to enhance the engagement?

With all the qualified or alleged contributions to DQ, it is essential to re-emphasize:

There is no DQ system or DQ management without DQ measurement.

4.1.3   Low awareness of the problem

DQ defects, consequences and expenses of their correction are not yet systematically gathered. Therefore the awareness of the problem is low. The slogan "what you don't know won't hurt you" seems to be at work and even questions concerning the sense of DQ measurements arise. The sense is reduced to a simple formula: increased credibility, reliability and trust.

In my view there is a parallel to the introduction of office copying machines in the middle of the last century. After the invention of the machines, the first Xerox salesmen were frequently asked why a company should buy or rent one of them. Despite all good arguments, the breakthrough for this technology took twelve long years. Nowadays no founder of a new company would turn down copy machines.

In Germany DQ is under discussion since the year 2000, i.e. for a good ten years by now. Very few companies have recognized the urgency of the topic and have set up a functioning DQ operation. If the mentioned parallel is applicable, the break through is imminent.

You might be right! I wish for you and for all of us that the DQ breakthrough will not take much longer. But please help me to better classify DQ thematically:

4.2   Thematic Crossovers

Which are the strongest contact points between DQ and other topics of organisation or IT?

Two contact points deserve special attention:

- Data management, specifically data organisation and

- ETL programming

The first point requires management attention, whereas a DQ manager usually can deal with the second.

4.2.1   „DQ management" versus „data management[8]"

From a superficial perspective, DQ management is unfortunately often held to be a better kind of "data management", characterised by an enhanced quality level. Data organisation concepts and tasks are presented as equivalents to DQ organisation and as must-have DQ activities.

Although similar in name, they belong to entirely different topics and share only a few overlaps. DQ is just a small facet of the higher-ranking concept of data management. Each topic can be pursued completely independent from the other, and not both of them have explicitly to be realised.

„Data management/data organisation" include as a superior concept all data-related aspects: data design (business and technical data modelling), data documentation, standardisation of essential information contents (e.g. customers, products, contracts, benefits), data access in programs, data transport (including ETL), data actualisation and release, authorisations, security aspects, release management procedures (in case the contents of important steering tables have been changed) and, of course, also DQ.

The implementation of a "data organisation system" resembles a reorganisation and potential restructuring of many business and technical data-related activities, and it pertains, to a great degree, to the IT organisation. DQ on the fringes of such a project could greatly complicate coordination and foster unwanted frictions. If there is already a

---

[8] In our context, data management is used as a synonym for master data management, data organisation and data governance.

functioning data organisation system, DQ can profit from its results and concentrate early on DQ measurements.

Congruency: in both approaches a central meta database is being utilized. However, DQ only requires a fraction of the functionality, which has to be assessed for data organisation. On the organisational level both share some role labels like data owner and data steward, referring to the operative DQ responsible employee or his representative.

Differences: are mainly to be found in the options for organisational embedding. A DQ team can be placed almost anywhere within an organisation, because its members need business as well as technical competences and a neutral status is intended anyway. Data management/-organisation requires high IT skills and should remain within the IT, despite strong interaction with business departments. Probably nobody would arrive at the idea to delegate the lead of data organisation to Intern Controlling or Risk Management.

If a DQ project is realised first, it should be include as few as possible aspects of data organisation. By following this strategy one can avoid data organisation matters infiltrating the project in undetected. Otherwise we would have to deal with unwanted internal disputes, delay of DQ results and aggravated acceptance of DQ.

My wishes in regard to DQ managers are, that first they should be successful in the field of DQ before getting involved in tasks of data organisation. Mixing both subject areas during the introduction stage is counter-productive. Verifiably successful DQ managers are best prepared for a leading position when a data organisation unit is established.

4.2.2   DQ Tools und ETL Programming

ETL programmers frequently react with insecurity in the course of the acquisition and introduction of DQ tools. For it becomes obvious at an early stage that the DQ tools provide some features which formerly had to be programmed with troublesome effort. Is everything now to be programmed differently or from scratch? Actually not! The following clarifications will help:

Data process security

This covers the guarantee that a data delivery is entirely processed and not repeatedly entered. That kind of guideline is part of ETL programming and generally does not require any business specifications. It is not an original function of a DQ tool. Here the most cost-effective and approved procedure should be adopted.

DQ rules

DQ rules require business specifications, which are applied during DQ check routines. The obtained results are to be archived in a central DQ results database. They provide the basis for the visualisation of DQ measurements. DQ check routines are provided by the DQ team and integrated into ETL processes by programmers.

In the realisation (implementation) of any other specifications for data cleansing and data enrichment and the like, programmers and their clients are principally free to choose the optimal way to proceed, and to choose tools to meet business requirements.

4.2.3 Data Process Security

Speaking of data process security, isn't that something with direct impact on DQ? Please, don't tell me the DQ team doesn't have anything to do with it!

Well, yes indeed! As auditor at the end of a DQ-R process (meaning DQ for regulatory purposes)!

DQ process security is a very important aspect. Recently it received new attention in connection with Solvency II. Because in the course of information extraction for the economical relevant key figures (e.g. following the data lineages) it has to be ensured that no information is lost. It must be made clear who is responsible and which procedures have to be activated in the case of a breakdown during data processing. And that might actually happen if you are relying on insufficient DQ. The required DQ process security may be rated as the last check (audit incl. report), which has to be carried out by the DQ team as soon as all DQ statements for the lineages of a financially relevant key figure are available.

4.3 Challenges in the Realisation Phase

Now let me ask some concluding questions to the expert: First I would like to know which are the largest and smallest obstacles that appear after the initialisation of a DQ project?

The largest and most persistent obstacle usually is the

establishment of a DQ controlling between transactional and reporting systems.

A moderate problem in the start phase might be the

allocation of data to data owners.

Rather harmless should be the clarification that

automatically produced results of a data profiling may not yet be
considered as results of a DQ measurement.

4.3.1   Introduction of a DQ Controlling Function

Just to refresh memory: DQ controlling means, for instance, that identified data sets with grave or suspicious DQ defects will be sorted out
during the data loading procedure. They are either sent back for correction to the data owner, or they are parked for manual inspection and
if necessary cleansing by the data owner or his representative. The
corrected and approved data will than be finally processed with the
next data load.

While loading data from production systems like a DWH, we occasionally encounter DQ monitoring routines. This means data sets with
suspicious and actual DQ defects are indeed identified and marked before loading, but then they are further processed as if everything was
correct. When indicated, the marked data sets are later checked and
corrected in the DWH.

One of the arguments in favour for this practice is that detected defects only affect a few users and other users simply cannot wait for the
corrections. Another argument is the narrow window (performance)
for the loading of data, which does not offer any chances for interrup-
tions. It is often acted in an archaic all-or-nothing manner. Either a de-
fect is detected and the whole data delivery is rejected or there are no
critical defects found and all is further processed. This is traditional
practice and well positioned in the minds of many employees.

Table 3: Effort for the recovery of data consistency at all levels

Production stage In which a defect is identified		Data defects correction effort	
		Increasing rate	Empirical values
Analysis layer	Front-Ends-Reports		≈ 24 PD[9] 10 - 40 PD
	x 10		
	Data Marts	↑	ca. 4,5 PD
Business layer	Data preparation		
	x 10		
Intelligence layer	Data Warehouse	↑	2 - 5 h.
	x 10		
Data layer / Staging area	Integration	↑	10 - 30 min.
	Data cleansing and transformation		
	x 10		
Source systems	Production data External data	↑	1 - 3 min.

What a pity, since we know from analyses that the time effort for the correction of data at the entry point is far less than at a later point in time, particularly after it has been submitted to several processing steps. The necessary time for corrections rises exponentially if defects become evident at or after publication. In the first case we will have correction times in the range of minutes (1-3 minutes), in the second case you will be confronted with an effort of several days (often 40 project days - see Table 3).

---

[9] PD = project day

Procedures for the later correction of "business data defects" within the DWH are also not trivial and require compromises in how they are to be handled.

Obstinately sticking to the above outlined practice diminishes a great deal of the DQM benefits. We still hope that it will be realised that the implementation of DQ controlling can be accomplished nowadays with much less effort than it took in past years. Some of the necessary functions, for instance notifications, parking and data release, are being provided by the new DQ tools and don't have to be programmed any longer.

It would be worthwhile to reconsider another series of technical and organisational options. A constructive collaboration between the DQ team, ETL programmers, data owners and selected data users would bring about highest benefits for all participants.

4.3.2   Attribution of data to the data owner

Although companies might already have established a clear attribution of applications to "functional responsible employees", the attribution of data owners to some data areas remains difficult.

But is this attribution really so important, that people have to rack their brains over it?

Oh yes, it is important to know who is responsible and makes the final decision as to whether abnormalities in the data are business relevant or not. It is also his decision whether and when DQ improvement actions will be carried out. So the data owner vitally determines the quality level of his data.

Without discussing this solvable topic in full length, here are three helpful notes:

-    Data owners are identified, not nominated,
-    There always is a data owner and
-    Data users become data owners as soon as they receive data from others and pass them on.

Who owns the data in a DWH, which many recipients have to rely on?

If there is no particular named "owner" of the data pools, the leading service provider responsible for the data supply in the DWH automatically has the data ownership toward his customers. Jestingly he might be called "data dealer". It would certainly be highly appreciated if he could stamp his data with a "DQ check approval seal", which informs the recipients about the DQ level. Thus they would know for what the data was tested and received approval.

4.3.3   Misunderstanding Data Profiling

Data profiling is not yet DQ measurement. For a start it yields a mix of statistical statements about the data. Every time you are confronted with such a pile of statistical information, it has to be analysed, interpreted and evaluated. That requires manual intervention and time. The evaluation of the analysis together with the data owner and optionally with the data users will then determine the further line of action. If the abnormalities in the data are classified as irrelevant for DQ, a DQ measurement will not be necessary. Only in this case, the data profiling report together with the DQ specialist's evaluation may be put on a level with the results of a DQ measurement.

Results of a DQ measure are clear without ambiguity, do not need further interpretation and hold an unmistakable evaluation. Just bear in mind: Data profiling is used to get acquainted with the data at the first encounter and to derive rules from this first contact, which will then be specifically analysed in the course of DQ measurements.

Alarm should be triggered as soon as manufacturers of data profiling tools emphasise the option to integrate data profiling into ETL programming. It is not reasonable to run a data profiling (meaning a repeated initial analysis) on every data transfer or data load. If the profiling tool does not support the analysis of individual DQ rules, it only signifies that nobody knows what to look for or which quality criteria should be applied. Sorry, I just don't understand the benefit of such "Alzheimer's routines"!

Your last comment is really interesting! It helps me to get along with some commentaries of our DQ specialists and enables me to pose some questions within the organisation in due time.

5 Factors for Success

Now, what are the most critical factors for the successful introduction of a DQ system?

The most critical factors for the successful introduction of a DQ system are directly associated with the DQ team.

Conceptual strength and processes competence

Should be on a high level within the DQ team. In a first step the processes to be supported by the DQ have to be mapped and agreed on. Together with the most important definitions, everything is put down in a preliminary DQ organisation handbook.

DQ organisation handbook

There a frame model for the collaboration of all parties is delineated and for this reason it is a central component of the DQ team's communication strategy. A quick outline of the handbook's first version is strongly recommended, so that all participants are informed about the line of action.

DQ competences

Every member of a DQ team should hold a minimum level of DQ competences and should be able to independently complete DQ check requests. A differentiation of tasks only makes sense after DQ competences have already been demonstrated. Otherwise the communication within the team is unnecessarily hampered. Also, historically grown competition between business departments and IT should be prevented from infiltrating the team.

Full-time employees in the DQ team

> Facing the new and complex tasks in a DQ team, it is rather unproductive to additionally entrust not yet fully incorporated DQ employees with DQ tasks. Generally such double pressure brings about harm to the DQ project, as well as to the employees. Members of a DQ team should have had at least 12 to 18 months of full-time experience as DQ specialists.

Quick to DQ measurements

> The quicker DQ measurements are realised and the sooner the team concentrates on concrete DQ results, the more professional and secure the actions of DQ team members will become.

Quick to DQ scorecards

> The acceptance of the data owners will grow along with the presentation of DQ results in the form of DQ scorecards for files or tables. DQ scorecards at the application or department level should begin much later, as already mentioned.

Focussing on DQ checks

> It is advisable to initially focus on the lineages of information retrieval for the most important business figures and on persistent DQ troubles.

Result orientation, pragmatism and patience

> Rome wasn't built in a day. Clearly laid out and objective DQ reports as well as steady attention to economical requirements are the last success factors I would like to mention. A general motto might be: Keep it simple!

6 Perspective

Thank you! Although all these new ideas and impressions still have to settle down, I would like to know what will be next, after we are through with DQ?

Oh, I'm sorry I didn't reach for my crystal ball this morning. If you want me to predict trends anyway, I can imagine that future developments will encompass the following:

DQ control centres

with overviews of the DQ network, with DQ monitoring, DQ controlling, DQ alerts and reasonable DQ performance times. I suppose that the increasing complexity of data landscapes and the present threat of no longer having adequately reliable data will enforce that kind of DQ control centre. For important documents/analysis we will have

DQ seals

in analogy to vehicle inspection stickers, guaranteeing a tested level of security or trust. Further, I am convinced, that in the context of quality offensives and process improvements

DQ indices as process performance indicators

will be developed, standing for the DQ adequate handling of data in processes and part processes. Their importance is going to increase in the course of time.

DQ check routines as single sources within the company

Last but not least, I envisage that eventually synergies between DQ, data organisation and application development will occur. That would be the case as soon as formerly defined DQ criteria for certain data (like customers, interested parties, products, contracts etc.) are centrally archived (single source) as a DQ check routine. Every programmer concerned with entry, support and transport of such data, can than include the central DQ check routines in his program. I predict that this will positively affect many steps of development. And please be assured that this is not just musing. Several DQ producers already present occasionally such SOA[10]-based solutions. But as we both know from experience, no matter how good these products may be, everything takes its time!

---

[10] SOA = Service Oriented Architecture

Epilogue

Now the CEO has a better basic concept for the classification of the data quality topic and is going to advise his colleagues at the management board not to postpone a DQ initiative indefinitely.

He will recommend a study, targeted at the identification of the necessary preconditions for a rapid implementation of a regular operating DQ system.

Although he does not believe that there are any significant DQ defects in his company, by now he wants to know it for sure! Especially since it helps to satisfy the financial regulators, investors and customers.

About the Author

Guilherme Morbey was born in 1956, in Lobito, Angola. After studying Computer Sciences in Germany he had his first work experience with IBM. They soon recognised and supported his consultation talent. Later he worked at a well renowned German consultancy and successfully managed several complex projects for corporate clients. Since 1998 he freelances as a consultant, mainly for financial service providers.

One of his thematic focuses since 2003 is the introduction of data quality management systems.

Contact
E-mail: guilherme@morbey.de
Website: www.morbey.de

Appendix

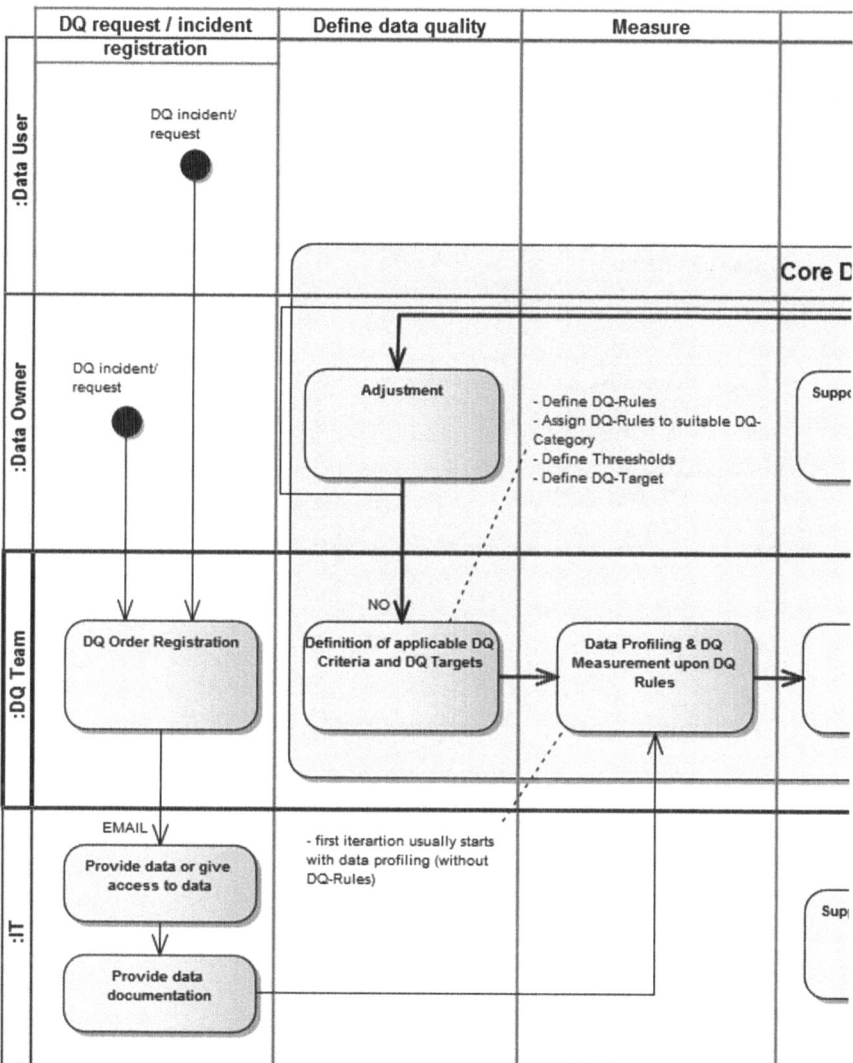

Figure 7:   General Data Quality Process (DQ-P)
Part 1 of 4

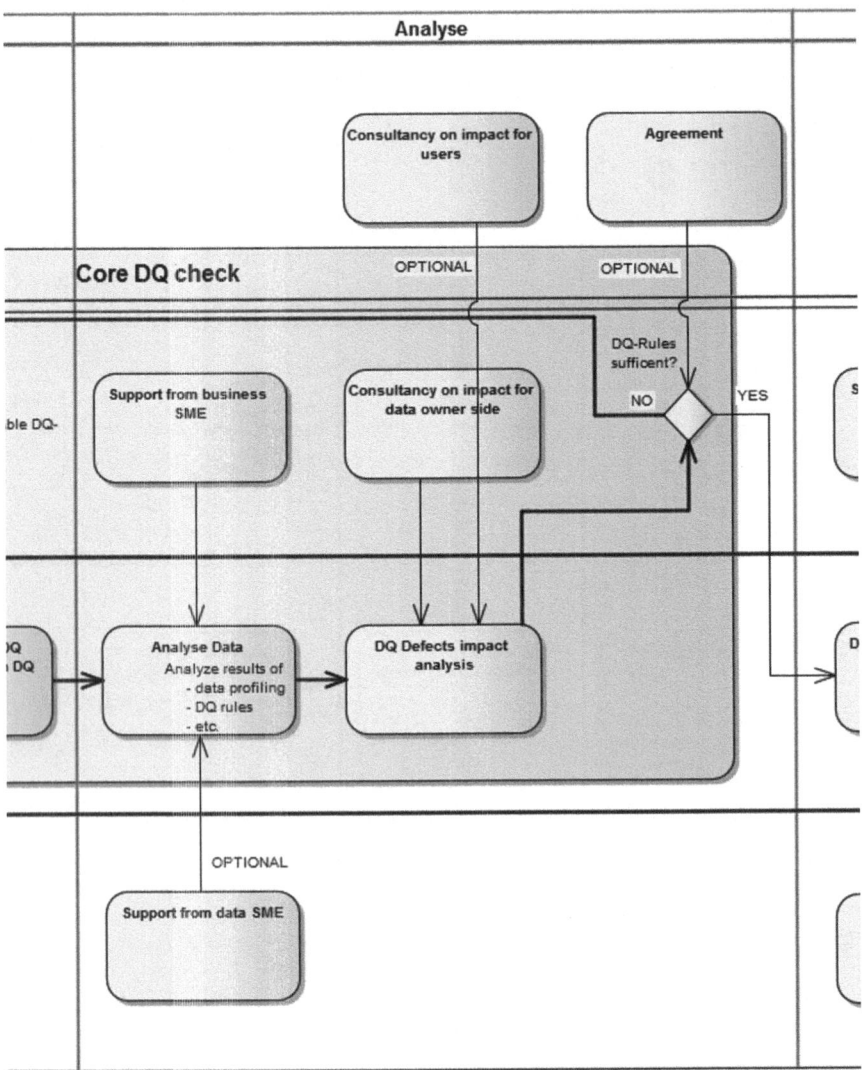

Figure 7: General Data Quality Process (DQ-P)
Part 2 of 4

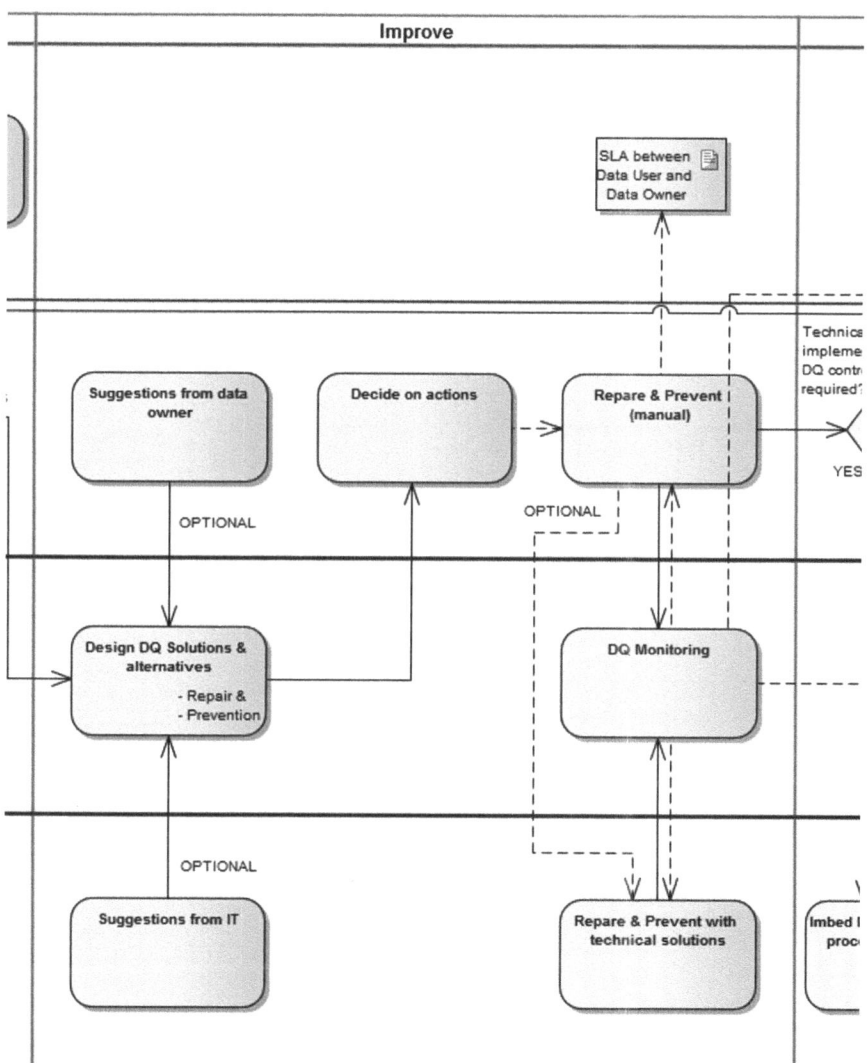

Figure 7:   General Data Quality Process (DQ-P)
                Part 3 of 4

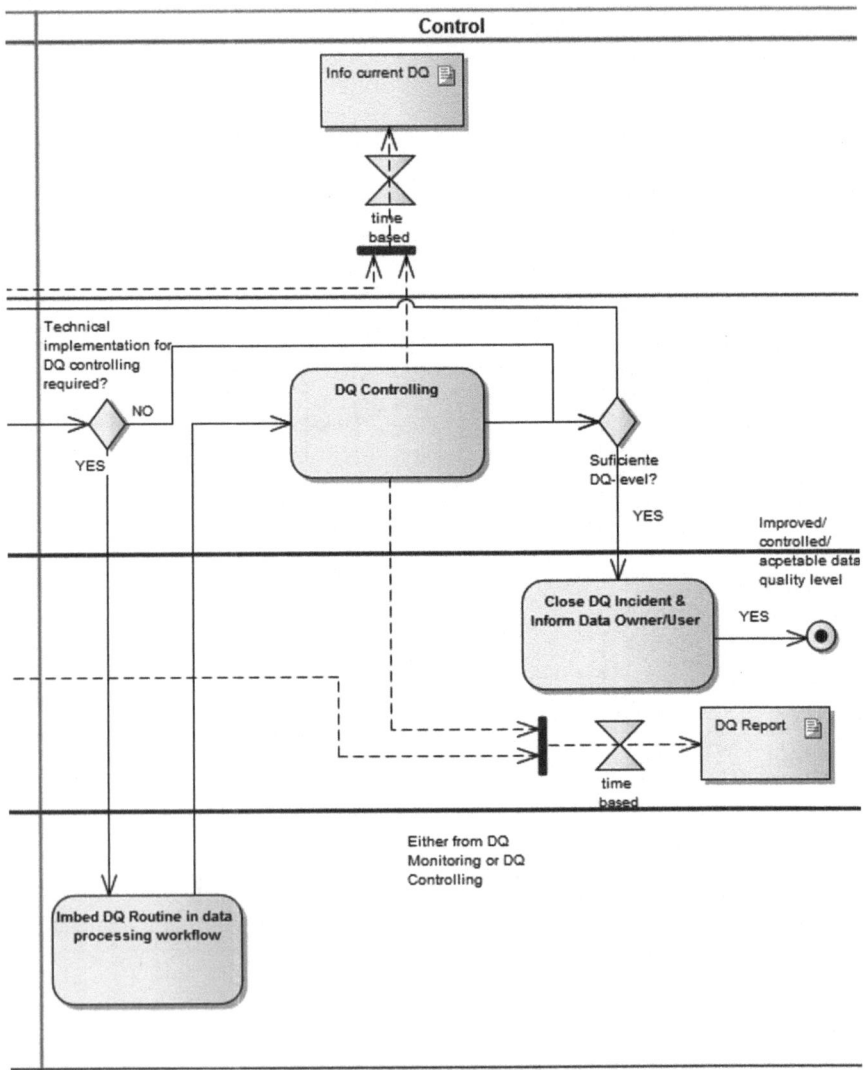

Figure 7:   General Data Quality Process (DQ-P)
                Part 4 of 4

Von der Promotion zum Buch

↗